Water, Ice, and Steam

Ira Wood

Rosen Classroom Books & Materials
New York

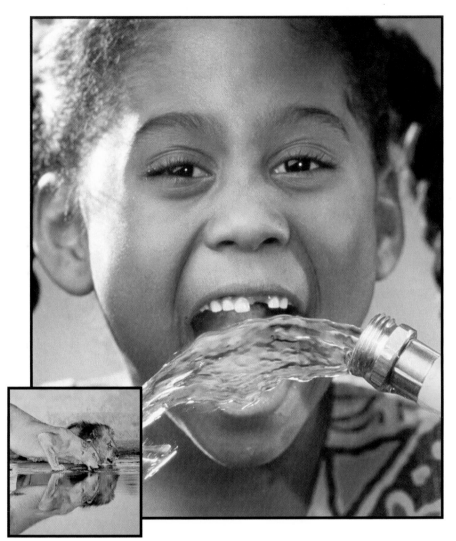

We need to drink water to live.
Plants and animals also need
water to live.

We use water to wash our hands
and bodies. We sometimes use
water to cook our food.

Rain is water that falls from
the sky. Rain fills our lakes
with water.

We can touch water, but we need to put it in a glass to hold it. .

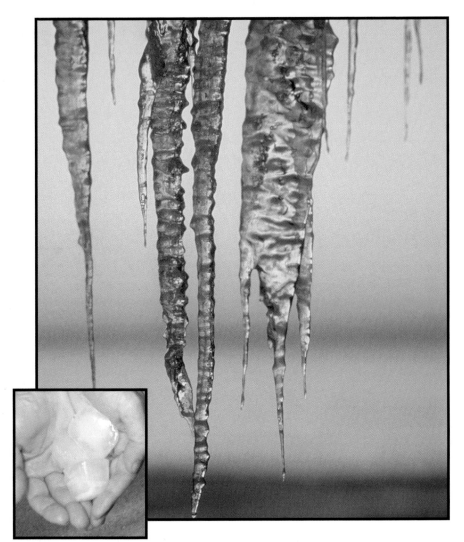

When water gets very cold, it turns into ice. We can hold ice in our hands.

When rain gets very cold, it turns
into snow. Snowflakes are made
of very small pieces of ice.

When ice warms up, it turns into water again.

Steam

When water gets very hot, it turns into steam. We can see steam, but we cannot hold it.

Steam

When we heat water on the stove, it turns into steam.

Water

When steam cools down, it turns
into water again.

Words to Know

lake

snowflakes

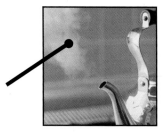

steam